I CAN HANDLE DIVORCE

Published By Rachael Alexander

CREDITS
Author: Rachael Alexander
Editor: Jo Watson-Davies
Design: Alistair Marshall (*yandi.co.uk*)
Photography: Unsplash
Editorial Assistants: Christine Fieldhouse, Helen Hunt, Ashlie Prescott *(much appreciated!)*

Published by

RA
Rachael Alexander

© 2014 I Can Handle It

www.rachael-alexander.co.uk
@icanhandleitUK

ALL RIGHTS RESERVED. This book contains material protected under international and Federal Copyright Laws and Treaties. Any unauthorized reprint or use of this material is prohibited. No part of this book may be reproduced or transmitted in any form or bay any means, electronic or mechanical, including photocopying, recording, or by any information storage and retrieval system without express written permission from the author / publisher.

PART OF THE *i can handle it!* FAMILY

Contents

1	I just want to live happily ever after!
2	Marriage is supposed to be hard work – isn't it?
3	I've got to make it work, I don't have a choice – do I?
4	I have to stay for the sake of my children – don't I?
5	I don't even know where to start
6	Solicitors and the court scare me
7	I don't want my children upsetting
8	Who will support me?
9	Why can't I stop crying?
10	I can handle making changes
11	I think I'm about ready
12	Helping others respect my life decision
13	Managing my ex partner
14	I can't survive on my own – can I?
15	Moving on – Bring it on!
16	OMG I've handled it!

DIVORCE

[dih-vawrs, -vohrs]
legally dissolve one's marriage with someone

This book is dedicated to...

my ex-husband who helped me to remember I always had the power,
I just had to learn it for myself. Thank You.

Other sources of inspiration in my life:
Since my own personal development journey started in 2000 there have been many inspirational authors, healers, mystics, family and friends who have helped me remember who I was born to be. Fortunately for me but unfortunately for you there are too many to list here.
However, I urge you to start to explore resources for yourself. I strongly recommend you to read any material by Susan Jeffers, Ph.D, Susan Forward, Ph.D, Beverley Engel and John Bradshaw. I thank these inspirational people who shared their wisdom and love with me. Locally I encourage you to ask the Universe to bring you the people you need to help guide you home.

"Home is a place that we must all find child. It's not just a place where you eat or sleep. Home is knowing. Knowing your mind, knowing your heart, knowing your courage. If we know ourselves, we're always home, anywhere"

Glinda the Good Witch – The Wiz (1978)
(Screenplay adapted from Frank L Baum novel
'The Wonderful Wizard of Oz' 1900)

Welcome to your new best friend - your I Can Handle... Divorce Journable

Your journable is a space where you can write your own ideas and thoughts down as you read the text. Writing down your ideas and thoughts is a healing process which will help you if you are feeling confused or uncertain over what action you need to take in your life at the moment.

Whether you decide to stay married, separate or divorce, you have to start somewhere and this journable will lead you through the process of making your decision. Please feel free to write, draw, doodle your way through this book. Many of us were taught not to write in books, but guess what, this book is "yours" so give yourself permission to write, doodle and draw as much as you want in it!

You can regard your journable as a private diary, which you can keep to yourself or you can choose to share the content with others. If you're having a difficult time, it will be a source of wisdom and comfort – a best friend who won't let you down. Feel free to read it and add to it as many times as you want. Keep it with you when you are going through this challenging time and it will never let you down, it's a constant reminder that you can handle it!

From one courageous heart to another

Rachael Alexander

In The Beginning

Some people commit to marriage truly believing it to be their best decision for them at the time, only for it to become a source of misery some way down the line.

This journable gives you advice and guidance to help you clarify your thinking about your marriage. What if you could be in a loving joyful relationship instead of an unhappy one? The biggest barrier to changing your life and being able to feel joy again is fear. The first thing you need to know is that fear is an illusion. Trust me when I tell you that you have got the courage to face anything in this life and you can do it. The first step is facing the truth about the situation, the second step is taking action, even just reading this journable will have a positive effect on your emotions as you are starting to confront the issue. The first step of improving a situation is to face it. Well done for being brave enough to admit there may be problems. I admire your bravery and courage. You have reconnected with the fearless and loving part of you which has always been inside of you and always will.

I know you can handle this... Be brave...

CHAPTER 1
I just want to live happily ever after!

Many people have their own ideas of what a 'happy marriage' should be like. We're brought up in the world of fairy tales, of meeting Prince Charming and Miss Right and for many of us the main aim in life becomes wanting to 'settle down and have a family'. Some of us are conditioned that we will only be 'happy' when we have found our life-partner, our 'soul mate'.

Some people do find that happiness and live a blissful life with the same person. However, maybe these fairytales have given us incorrect ideas. Maybe we can spend our life with more than one person. Maybe the real point of relationships is to help each other become a more loving, compassionate, fearless soul living with an opening heart which benefits ourselves and others. I believe different relationships in our lives help us to achieve this if we commit to our spiritual growth and see relationships as a source of helping our soul to heal and learn from life experiences.

If our daily life living with another person is filled with tension, arguments, resentment and bitterness then this can affect our mental health. It can also have a negative effect on the mental health of children living with us which can then affect their life when they are an adult. If you are unhappy; think about what messages you are giving to your children about 'marriage and relationships'. Do you really want them to be adults living like this in 20 years?

✏️ So let's take a look at what makes a happy marriage or healthy relationship: Please feel free to tick the box if your marriage or relationship has each element.

- [ ] You are enjoying sharing your life with a supportive partner who listens to you, encourages you, and wants you to succeed in all areas of life.
- [ ] You share responsibility for creating a positive environment through positive loving words and actions.
- [ ] Do things to make each other happy and to live an easier life.
- [ ] Show care and consideration for each other and the rest of the family.
- [ ] Keep promises and commitments to situations and events.
- [ ] Not say cruel things, laughing at, or belittling each other.
- [ ] Are honest and open in communications with each other.
- [ ] Think of each other's needs, not just your own.
- [ ] Are prepared to compromise in situations, so both partners are happy.
- [ ] Encourage each other to rest when you need to and being prepared to take up the slack.
- [ ] Share the burden of household chores and family responsibilities.
- [ ] Able to have honest and calm conversations to arrive at a compromise.
- [ ] Are financially open and working together to manage the family finances.
- [ ] Respect each other and celebrate your achievements.

Add your ideas here how you would like your marriage to be

I want my marriage / relationship to be...

e.g. I want my marriage to stop being a battle ground and we work together more sharing responsibilities. I want it to be more about compromise than arguing and hate feeling like I am walking on eggshells when she walks in the door. I want a positive environment for me and the kids.

CHAPTER 2
Marriage is supposed to be hard work - isn't it?

After completing the list, you may have realised that your marriage could be better. Many people believe that there's no such thing as a 'happy marriage' and that no relationship can be equally happy for both partners, all of the time. This may be true, but two people who love each other usually want each other to be happy. Disagreements will arise, but it's how we work together to overcome them that's important.

Sometimes when the love fades in a relationship, resentment and bitterness take over. Faced with this situation, we may be fearful to break up because we have been in the relationship for a long time and it may be all we know. We may simply be fearful about being on our own.

It's common to hear "I do love him/her, but I'm not in love with him/her". This can often mean, the familiarity and comfort of being with this person overrides our fear of being on our own. Sometimes we may not want to end the marriage as we believe we love the other person so much. Whilst this may be true it is also important we receive love back, not just occasionally or when he or she does a nice thing for us. A loving relationship is not one where we spend more time upset and angry than feeling relaxed and positive. Unfortunately some people have rarely had a loving relationship role modelled in their past so we struggle to know what one looks like.

Apart from facing our fear, we may also have to challenge our own and society's belief system about what we think marriage is.

You often hear people say:

- But marriage is supposed to be hard work.
- No relationship is perfect all of the time, that's not realistic.
- It's healthy to have a good argument.
- I took my vows in church and I can't go against them.
- My parents made it work, so I must too.
- It is not realistic to think we can be happy all the time.

These are examples of **beliefs** that get passed down the generations as being the "right thing" or the "done thing". Today's reality is that we are fortunate enough to live differently to past generations and we can make our own decisions about our own lives and what makes us happy.

It is important that we are able to explore our beliefs. We copy our beliefs from society, past generations, the media, our friends and the way we were brought up. Beliefs are a way of thinking we take as the truth, however I personally believe it is important we use our free will to choose how to live rather than how tradition dictates we should live. Some of us were brought up very traditionally and we feel we will be wrong if we break tradition. I believe to live your life lovingly rather than out of fear, guilt and tradition* is more important – don't you?

---

* Tradition: Transmission of beliefs passed from one generation to another

Let us now explore your beliefs and traditions. Complete the sentences with the first response that comes to mind.

Remember these beliefs and traditions may not belong in your life right here right now

Marriage is... *e.g. Hard work*

Being married means... *e.g. Security*

A husband should... *e.g. Look after me*

A wife should... *e.g. Look after me*

Ending a marriage is*... *e.g. Wrong*   **Because...** *e.g. I will have failed*

What I really want do now is *e.g. Pull the duvet over my head*

Are the answers you wrote your 'truths' or are they outdated beliefs passed down from older generations?

icanhandle **DIVORCE**

CHAPTER 3
I've got to make it work, I don't have a choice - do I?

By now, you may be thinking that your relationship could be different and you may have to make choices that will change the status quo. By taking action, things may get more challenging before they get better, but not taking any action could make the situation worse still as nothing will improve.

Many of us believe we have to stay as we don't have a choice. The reasons for believing we have to stay in the relationship could be:

- Financial reasons.
- Have children who you believe will be upset if you separate.
- Have pets which you don't want to lose.
- Have a house which may have to be sold.
- Have cars on the drive which you may lose.
- Have friends who are in couples, so it will make socialising difficult.
- Can't afford to split up as no equity in the house.
- You wouldn't like to be single.
- Separating may upset parents, friends and family.
- Feel embarrassed that you have 'failed' if you leave.
- Don't want the emotional upheaval.
- Don't know where to start - it's too overwhelming.

Whilst some reasons may be reality, there is always a way that we can improve a situation. It just often means there may be some tough decisions and sacrifices that we have to make which may affect ourselves and others. However, knowing we can handle the tough times makes us stronger inside, which reduces the anxiety and stress that we can feel sometimes.

It is not always about ending the relationship and getting a divorce. There are other choices available that you could consider.

What are your choices?

- You could talk to your partner about how you're feeling and ask them if they feel the same.
- You could talk to your partner about going for counselling together.
- You could go to counselling on your own.
- You could speak to friends who are divorced for their reality of life.
- You could start to live separate lives.
- You could ignore the situation and pretend it's ok – put up and shut up.
- You could continue to think that marriage is all about arguing, moaning and sulking.
- You could start to have an affair or continue with an affair.
- You could hope your partner will change.
- You could accept that he or she will never change but this means stopping complaining about them.
- You could push everything under the hypothetical carpet and ignore how you feel.

✎ Look back at the choices on page 21 and consider each one in turn. There may be one or two that are more appealing than the others.

What do you think about the choices available?

e.g. I could do some of them

Does one jump out more than any others?

e.g. Go for counselling

Write down the ones that you may consider....

e.g. Talk to my partner about going for counselling

Which one scares you the most?

e.g. Talking to her about it, she may get angry

Please don't feel overwhelmed at this point. You are only thinking about the different options available. You are being really brave in dealing with the situation. Many people choose not to face challenging situations, yet here you are ready to think about it. That is courage. You can do this, don't stop now. Remember fear is an illusion.

When we start to think about making changes in our life, the fearful part of us will try and stop us as it is scared of the unknown. Our body tries to stop us by pumping adrenalin through our body which can make us feel physically ill. Facing our fear helps us to become loving to ourselves and others – I believe this is the spiritual journey. The option which scares us the most is usually the path we need to follow to reach inner peace.

Some say **FEAR** stands for

Fake **E**verything **A**ppear **R**eal

You brush all your problems under the carpet where the problem stays and the unhappiness festers. You are lying to yourself and the other people such as your children who will pick up on it.

Or it can mean...

Face **E**verything **A**nd **R**ise

You find the courage to make life better for yourself and take action to make it better. You may have some emotional turbulence but you eventually find peace. It is very rare to hear people say; "I wish I'd never separated". It is more common to hear; "I never looked back". You have a right to live in a non-hostile environment.

When we show ourselves we can face our fear, a part of us psychologically matures and we eliminate some of our fear. This makes us able to face challenges in the future.

YOU DESERVE TO HAVE HAPPINESS IN YOUR LIFE

you can handle it!

What do you think you are doing right now reading this journable?

Circle your answer...

Faking it?   Facing it?

Yes, you are facing it and you will rise one day, stronger, more empowered and happier. We have all faked our happiness at some point - it is part of being human. Comfort the scared part of you and commit to honouring the way you really feel from today. You can handle it!

CHAPTER 4
I have to stay for the sake of my children - don't I?

It's understandable that you will have fear – you're human! However, we often make excuses so that we don't have to face the fear, change our routine or disrupt the status quo. **This is the power of fear!**

When we've been in the same situation or routine for a long time, we think it feels safe and secure, but it may not be bringing us happiness. We need to find the courage to make a change. Our beliefs are so hard wired we think we are behaving in the best way for our happiness. Until someone points this out to us, we rarely think life can be any different.

Remember our beliefs are based on the ways we've been conditioned to think from our past, they may be based on others opinions and they can be holding us back. Some people do not move with the times and stay living as our grandparents lived in the past. Fortunately the law and human rights have changed allowing us to make life choices which can make us happier.

We all need help from other people who have often been through the journey themselves. I can only write this book as I have been through the journey and I know how scary it is, yet I also know how much more emotionally resilient I am now and I am learning I can handle anything that comes my way.

I recommend you read *Feel the Fear and Do it Anyway*® by Dr Susan Jeffers. It certainly changed my life and I hope it changes yours.

What do you think are some of your beliefs about ending your marriage?

Tick the boxes you agree with.

- [ ] I will have failed.
- [ ] My children will be affected emotionally.
- [ ] It's unfair of me to break up the family home.
- [ ] My parents will be disappointed in me.
- [ ] I won't be able to afford it.
- [ ] I don't know where to start.
- [ ] He or she may get violent.
- [ ] I can't manage on my own.
- [ ] I will be lonely and I won't be able to cope.
- [ ] I will upset the other person.
- [ ] I will be criticised.
- [ ] My children will never forgive me.
- [ ] I will never see my children again.

Add any other ideas here

e.g. What if I never meet anyone again

....

....

....

✏️ Start to challenge the beliefs you have ticked. Pretend you have to prove what you have ticked is wrong - what will you say to disprove these beliefs?

e.g. how do you know you can't manage on your own or how do you know you can't afford it?

....

....

....

....

....

....

....

> Struggling to disprove your fearful beliefs? Imagine 'worry' and 'courage' are two people stood in front of you. Ask yourself what would worry say to you and what would courage say to you? Courage is the voice to listen to as worry is fear and fear is an illusion. You can handle anything!

Isn't it frightening that our beliefs are so powerful, as we think they are the absolute 'truths' of a situation. It is only when we speak to other people, read books and gain further insight that we often change our opinions and beliefs on a situation. This is called raising our consciousness and brings us more rewarding thoughts, feelings and behaviour reducing mental health problems or addiction to drinking, drugs or eating. Remember we can have different beliefs to others, especially our parents and grandparents.

Write here who or what can help you challenge your way of thinking about this situation.

e.g. my best friend, see a counsellor

....

....

....

You may have written seeing a counsellor, visiting a library, going online to read blogs or even talking to a trusted colleague about how you feel. This is excellent as you are showing you can accept help which is a courageous act. Well Done!

CHAPTER 5
I don't even know where to start

You may have tried speaking to your partner and it may have resolved things, which is great. Well done for taking action, but the fact that you're reading this book suggests that there is still some doubt in your mind.

Maybe you want to talk again, but your partner is in denial about the situation and doesn't want to face it. If they're not willing to talk about it, then unfortunately there's nothing you can do. However think about what message this is giving, and why he or she refuses to do this. If they truly wanted to get the relationship back on track, wouldn't they go to counselling, wouldn't they do anything to make this work?

It's understandable you may have fear about confronting the issues, however nothing will change without change. Remember, you can always go for counselling on your own to help you deal with the situation. You may be at a point where separation is the only option but you may have fears about where to start.

If you are thinking of separating then your starting point could be to explore the different options open to you. The option you chose will depend on many factors including the amicability of your relationship and financial situation. Search options available to you. i.e. Google Arbitration, Marriage, Leeds.

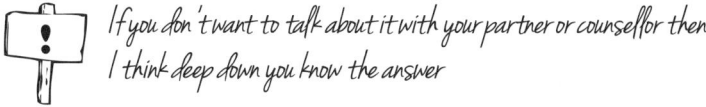

If you don't want to talk about it with your partner or counsellor then I think deep down you know the answer

Options include:

- **Mediation:** These sessions are held by a qualified mediator who helps you to both agree on the practical arrangements including what's best for your children if you have any, and sorting out the financial considerations.
- **Collaborative Law:** You both sit with your respective solicitors around a table and everything is discussed in the open.
- **Arbitration:** A qualified solicitor arbitrates the situation between both parties, which avoids racking up legal bills.
- **Court:** This can be the most expensive option and a 'last resort'; however it's sometimes needed if one party doesn't want to keep the situation amicable.
- **A Solicitor:** A solicitor can help you decide which is the best option for you. Ask friends to recommend solicitors or look in the phone book and ask about costs upfront.
- **A Non-Practicing Solicitor:** This is a solicitor who can act on your behalf, they can advise you of the differences to a solicitor. Ask about costs upfront.
- **Do It Yourself:** You can separate and conduct your own legal separation. The internet will advise you of different options.

THE DAY I REALISED I HAD A RIGHT TO BE HAPPY WAS THE DAY I WALKED FREE

Rachael Alexander

CHAPTER 6
Solicitors and the court scare me

Many people don't like to include solicitors however if there is money involved such as a shared house or children then it is recommended. Remember just because you ask a solicitors advice doesn't mean you have to get divorced. You are just getting information to help make you make your decision. Knowledge is power!

It's important that you trust your legal representative. This person fully understands the legal process and you don't as it is complex. You wouldn't try to fix a leaking roof, you would leave it to an expert.

Like any relationship you have to manage it. The first time you meet your legal representative, see how you connect with him or her. Do you feel safe, cared for and in the right hands? Do not be afraid of seeing a few until you feel that this person will support you in this life transition.

Remember
- Your solicitor is your legal representative not your best friend. Their job is to get you the best financial deal and the best arrangements for your children. They're not your punch bag, counsellor, mother, therapist, father, partner or enemy. They have your best interests at heart, even if sometimes you may not think so.

- You don't have to be represented by someone who agrees with the legal system, but you do have to be represented by someone who understands it inside out. The legal system is there to sort out the division of money and decide what's in the best interests of any children based on a series of assumptions. It's a process that has to be gone through and you need an excellent guide.

- Divorce or separation can sometimes get challenging between two parties. There will be times when your legal representative has to intervene and go to court on your behalf, maybe to get an injunction to protect your children for example. You can help your legal representative by not only telling the truth, but also by keeping it factual and real. The case they put together to fight for what is right for you is based on your 'truth'. Leave the emotion and drama for your friends and your counsellor. For every minute you are crying, shouting, sulking, moaning, it's costing you money and clouding your thinking.

- A good legal representative will show you empathy but will also keep you focused on the task in hand. Use your legal representative to sort out the legal issues and your counsellor to help you manage psychologically and emotionally. Remember, the legal process provides you with protection should your ex-partner become unreasonable or threatening. Orders can be obtained from the court to stop this behaviour even if it is purely mental and emotional harassment. The police can also be involved to stop pestering. Legal aid can often be obtained where there is domestic abuse.

What are the things that are worrying you that you need to ask your solicitor?

e.g. Write here anything you want to ask your solicitor, you may want to ask about; timeframes, cost, contacting them, paperwork, splitting up pets/household

When and how will you take action to find legal support?

e.g. I will Google Solicitors by Wednesday

CHAPTER 7
I don't want my children upsetting

Where children are involved this is when you are responsible for making it a smooth transition. Here are some suggestions to make it easier on the children reducing negative impact on their mental health.

- Where possible it's better if both parents tell the children about the separation, together. Speak to the children on a Saturday morning so they have all weekend to ask questions or be upset. Let them be upset - lots of hugs.
- Make it clear that their behaviour is not connected to the cause of the separation, explain separation often happens in families.
- Make it clear that they are loved by both of you, and that will never change.
- Tell school what's happening and keep them informed so they can keep an eye on the children.
- If the school offers counselling, encourage your child to take it.
- Encourage them to ask you any questions which may worry them.
- Explain life will be different, no better, no worse, just different for them.
- Encourage them to talk about how they are feeling, even draw pictures to help them express their feelings.
- Keep all channels of communication open between you all.
- Do not use your children as emotional weapons and put them in the middle, they will only resent you when they are older.

The separation may prove challenging for you all. However the responsibility of a parent is to reduce the impact on the child as much as possible. Sometimes this will be challenging for you. Please don't worry if your child catches you crying, explain this is a normal human reaction when we are upset and tears are meant to be shed, just like going to the toilet. It means we are letting go of the past and starting to heal.

These following ideas are key to helping your child and you in the long run.

- Use ways to keep communication open with your ex. One strategy is to use a note book that goes backwards and forwards.
- Never use the children as weapons to get back at your partner, even if your ex tries to use them in that way.
- Keep the mental and emotional welfare of your children as your top priority and maintain your honesty and dignity, even if your former partner doesn't.
- Do not lie to your children about the situation as they will learn to distrust you. However speak to them in an age appropriate way.

Unless your children are over 18 sometimes they are too young to understand why a relationship or marriage has to end. However as they grow older, they will learn to understand. There are many wonderful books to help you, such as *'The Boys & Girls Guide To Divorce'* by Richard Gardner. Never be afraid to encourage your child to see a counsellor to help them through this life changing situation. It will help them in years to come to form positive relationships. Please don't feel guilty about separating. When you got married and had children, you made the right decision for you at the time. Life is about change.

CHAPTER 8
Who will support me?

Your children (or even parents) may try to manipulate you by saying they will disown you if you don't return to the family home or try to repair the marriage. This is their fear and they may try to do anything to make you stay together. It is important you recognise you are important enough to give yourself permission to make decisions which are right for you.

Your parents or children are not living your life so they cannot understand what your unhappiness feels like. Encourage your children or parents to have counselling to help them deal with their own thoughts and fears. Remember you have a right to be happy.

Write any concerns you may have about your children or your parents reactions

e.g. Parents are angry I am separating

....

....

Write here any action you will take to resolve these concerns

e.g. Empathise with how they feel, they are from a different generation

....

....

CHILDREN NEED A POSITIVE ENVIRONMENT TO FLOURISH WHETHER IT BE TRADITIONAL OR NOT

CHAPTER 9
Why can't I stop crying?

The greatest gift you can give yourself is to grieve the end of your relationship. You will suffer loss on every level. If this choice was forced upon you, you will face a huge sense of loss, particularly if you didn't see it coming and/or you didn't want it to end. Even if you are the one who chose to end the marriage, it is still a loss and you still need to give yourself permission to grieve.

If you give yourself permission, you may find yourself crying over:

- How challenging this separation process is.
- Loosing your future together.
- Loosing out on future years of family life together.
- Loosing feelings of being so in love when you married.
- Wondering why you stayed unhappy for so long.
- Wondering why you didn't put your happiness as a priority all those years ago.
- Angry that your children are from a *'broken home'.
- Realising that he or she wasn't willing to change to make things better.

*Broken home – Research shows that if children witness contempt, silence, anger, bitterness and resentment, they can suffer effects more than being raised in a home with one parent of love, kindness, consideration and respect.

(National Scientific Council on the Developing Child. (2005/2014). Excessive Stress Disrupts the Architecture of the Developing Brain: Working Paper 3. Updated Edition.)

As the process continues, you may cry over

- Instability of losing a home or the financial pressures.
- Dealing with the (repeated) questions a child asks about why you had to split up.
- Anger that you only wanted to get married once and stay married.
- How your partner is treating you through the divorce, when once upon a time you were madly in love.
- How your family may take your partner's side.
- Realisation that the relationships you had together with friends, in-laws or stepchildren will never be the same again.

The best way to deal with this is just to let yourself cry, so buy a supply of tissues and warn people that you may cry, a lot. This is all part of the process, just as much as selling the house and sorting out access arrangements for your children is. Crying is a normal human reaction. You may end up crying at times when you don't really understand why you are crying – for example, watching a movie where a family seem happy together. This is natural and part of the grief process. One day you may be able to look back and remember the good times.

CHAPTER 10
I can handle making changes

When we are facing any life change, it is important to be aware of the different stages and to recognise which stage we are in as this then allows you to keep focused on the next step. There are many wonderful books written on how to manage loss and change. The library and internet will also be a valuable source of wisdom. It is important to give yourself time to grieve the changes too. Tears and upset are a good sign that you are moving through the stages.

Which stage do you think you are at?

e.g. Frustration - Sulking and silent treatment

How can you move to the next stage?

e.g. Admit something has to change

Forgiveness & compassion for self and others. Unconditional love

Action 🔟
Take steps to improve the situation and situation starts to change.

Take Responsibility ⑧
I can do something to change this situation, nobody else can.

Acceptance ⑥
I have to do something and change. Allow emotions to be discharged. Then its upwards if we draw on.

⑨ Trust & Accept Help
Trust in self and accept help from others, have faith in the Universe to help.

⑦ Courage
Believe I have a right to happiness and I can change things.

Can keep getting stuck and going round and round at this point and start to feel frustration again, or can go to next step...

Emotional ⑤
Anger, upset, anxious, obsessive thoughts, low mood.

Confusion ③
Why am I feeling like this, its not right?

Frustration ①
Annoyance, moaning/groaning, emotional turmoil.

④ Denial/Blame
I can't change this situation – its them not me that have created this.

② Rock Bottom
Something has to change - I can't go on like this or my mental health will start to suffer.

Fear

CHAPTER 11
I think I'm about ready

Reading all the above and how it may affect you emotionally may make you think it will be less stressful if you stay together. At the end of the day this is your choice. In reality who would want to face all the above pain? However, please remember the amount of time you spend crying will be much less than the amount of time you have been spending complaining about your partner or dealing with the emotional ups and downs that an unhappy marriage brings. You will also have times of laughing, feeling relaxed and enjoying the new freedom that your new life will bring.

The process of divorce can be long and laborious, emotional and challenging and will seem as though it never ends. You can let it destroy your life or let it define you. This means you can use this experience to be stronger, more courageous and stand up for your rights, or you can crawl into a corner, give up and submit to your ex's demands. This latter option is a choice you have to make, but be warned that in years to come, when you feel stronger, you may have resentment and bitterness that you didn't fight for what you wanted due to not wanting to face it.

Many who have been through the separation and divorce process will some days have felt the following and you will too. It is a normal human reaction that you will feel like:

- You want to give in.
- You want to glve up.
- You want to stay in bed.
- You want to give up work.
- You wonder if you have done the right thing.
- You want to give him or her everything.
- You want to give him or her nothing.
- You want someone to take away the pain.
- You don't want to make decisions.
- You wish it would all go away.
- You wish someone would come and make it all better.
- You want to go back to them.

You can and will face this. You will survive this and you will come out stronger, both mentally and emotionally ready to move on with your life

Write here how else you are feeling

e.g. Tired, stressed and fed up

....

....

....

....*...its ok to feel this way*

I WAITED SO LONG FOR HIM TO CHANGE – WHAT I DIDN'T REALISE IS IN ORDER FOR HIM TO CHANGE, I HAD TO BE THE ONE TO CHANGE. LIKE A CATERPILLAR EMERGING FROM THE COCOON I FOUND MY WINGS

CHAPTER 12
Helping others respect my life decision

Only you can dig deep to find the courage to protect your future and your children's future. I know you can and will handle it. Remember the more you handle it, the stronger you will start to feel internally as you are showing your fearful side that there is nothing to fear. Fear is an aspect of your personality, not the whole of you.

So commit to it 100%. Commit 100% of your time and energy in trying to resolve the process. If you do this, you'll know that you tried your best, even if a legal decision is made that you don't agree with or the outcome is not as you hoped. Sometimes standing up and fighting for what you believe in is justice in itself. Only then will you have no lasting regrets, bitterness or anger and you won't wish you'd done more or done things differently. This will then allow you to let go and move on, ready for the next exciting chapter in your life. It is also important you have people in your life who you can lean on for emotional support.

Write here who can support you whilst going through this process......

e.g. My friends

You may be starting to feel that separation is the right decision for you at this point in your life. However, just because you are happy with moving on others may not be so. All of a sudden the following people may start to feel threatened by your new-found courage.

- Your parents, family and extended family.
- Your friends.
- Your work colleagues.
- Your in-laws.
- Your children.
- Your soon to be ex-partner.
- Your church or religious faith.

Whilst others may feel as though they have a right to give their opinions and thoughts - remember this is your life not theirs. You may have sparked some fear in them but the fears belong to them, not you, so don't take their fear and start wearing it yourself.

Remember, You can thank them for their concern but as it is your life you will make the right decisions for you and your family

Who may be upset about my decision?

e.g. Children / Parents

How can I remain strong and not feel guilty about my decision?

e.g. Repeat I have a right to be happy and want them to know what a loving relationship is

How will I respond when they tell me I shouldn't be doing this?

e.g. I will understand their belief system is in operation and their beliefs belong to their generation

Who can I turn to who will be on my side?

e.g. My counsellor and best friend

CHAPTER 13
Managing my ex-partner

Next to you, the person who may feel the most hurt is probably your ex-partner if he or she didn't want it. It's a sad fact when people are hurt they can act out their anger, become defensive and try to hurt you emotionally, mentally and sometimes physically, remember hurt people hurt.

Your ex-partner may:

- Get angry and shout at you.
- Harrass you with abusive texts and emails.
- Try and call repeatedly.
- Cry and beg you to take them back.
- Promise he/she will change.
- Try to threaten you with not seeing the children.
- Threaten to leave you homeless/carless/moneyless.
- Threaten legal action.

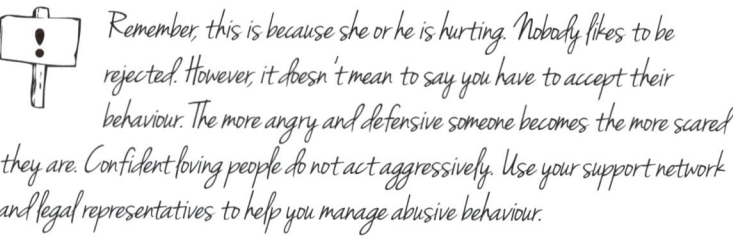

Remember, this is because she or he is hurting. Nobody likes to be rejected. However, it doesn't mean to say you have to accept their behaviour. The more angry and defensive someone becomes the more scared they are. Confident loving people do not act aggressively. Use your support network and legal representatives to help you manage abusive behaviour.

I have a right to
be happy...
This too shall pass
I have a right to
be happy...
This too shall pass

You will have times when communicating with your ex will make you feel overwhelmed and upset. The stronger you become internally and believe that you have a right to this life choice will help you act with dignity, courage and eventually compassion towards him or her.

Here are some techniques for managing communications with your ex.

- Receive advice on how to set boundaries with your ex. Ask your legal team or the internet will have articles on how to set boundaries or if to respond at all.
- Inform your ex how you would like to receive communications from them. Preferred method may be email or letter or even via your solicitor. You can then choose when to read them.
- Keep copies of the correspondence and if they become abusive speak to the police or your legal team.
- If you receive threatening communication, remember you don't have to reply straight way. Give yourself time to calm down, express your anger in a notebook which is just for you to read and then when you feel ready to reply ask yourself: What would courage write back kindly but assertively?
- Remember you don't have to do what they demand, you can say No, with no justification needed.

Remember you do not have to give in to their demands, no matter how much they bully you. You can and will handle this, however remember you can ask others to intervene to help. Sometimes bullies need a perceived higher authority to stop them bullying.

CHAPTER 14
I can't survive on my own - can I?

So when the times get particularly tough how can you handle it? Firstly be realistic. You will have challenging days. You'll also have days when you feel free, alive and ready to take on the world, thankful you have got out of your unhappy relationship. Embrace these days.

Have your coping strategies set up and ready to put into action for when the tough days kick in. Tick the ones you could consider doing.

- [ ] Join a gym. Even if you do nothing more strenuous than sitting in the jacuzzi and steam room, it will help you to relax.
- [ ] Take a walk. Fresh air and deep breaths help calm an anxious mind.
- [ ] Try downloading a meditation app or buy a meditation CD or DVD.
- [ ] Take up yoga, golf, pilates or body balance or any other activity that will help your mind to de-stress.
- [ ] Buy other 'I Can Handle...' Journables.
- [ ] Meet with positive friends who lift your mood.
- [ ] Read self-help books from the library.
- [ ] Buy self-help books from shops or online.
- [ ] Watch inspirational true story films.

- [ ] Avoid news broadcasts or depressing programmes like soap operas.
- [ ] Follow positive people on facebook or twitter.
- [ ] Seek spiritual help, whether it be through the church or by seeing a healer.
- [ ] Speak nicely to yourself and avoid people who add to your negative state.
- [ ] Have fun with your children; scrap modelling, living room picnics and armchair dens are fun and inexpensive.
- [ ] Take up new hobbies or study for a new qualification.
- [ ] Reconnect with old friends or make new friends.
- [ ] Become a volunteer for a cause close to your heart.
- [ ] Be open to alternative therapies like counselling or Reiki healing.

Add your own ideas here...

e.g. I can think of what my dear old Gran would have said to me

....

....

....

....

....

You'll have days when you feel alone and that no one understands what you're going through. Learn to accept these feelings of loneliness; you will get used to being on your own and making your own decisions. Over time, loneliness won't be an issue and you will enjoy being on your own.

CHAPTER 15
Moving on - Bring it on!

The most beautiful thing about divorce is being able to move on and start a new chapter in your life.

A chapter of :

- Learning to meet your own needs.
- Reduced conflict, tension, arguments and strife.
- Learning what a loving relationship is all about.
- Realising how strong you were all along by being able to handle the divorce process.
- Showing others that there is life after divorce and an unhappy marriage.
- Educating your children that life without both mum and dad is not worse, it's just different.
- Embracing your courage that you can handle being on your own or learning to love again.
- Realising that freedom is being able to decide what you want to do, when you want to do it and with whom.
- Exploring your sexuality.
- Healing your past.
- Learning to love and respect yourself.
- Learning what you want and need from new relationships that come into your life.
- Teaching your children how to build their self-confidence.

Write down what your new exciting chapter could hold for you...

I could...
e.g. Go out when I want to go out

I will...
e.g. Turn my house into a home, install a huge TV in/have pink cushions

I have always wanted to...
e.g. Go travelling

I won't miss...
e.g. The arguments

Before I had my partner, I used to enjoy...
e.g. My own time.

Balancing out the difficult days will be the fantastic days when you can make decisions regarding:

- Where you want to eat.
- What you want to eat.
- Who you want to spend time with.
- What you want to spend time doing.
- What holidays you want to go on.
- What you want to do on a weekend.
- What you want to spend your money on.
- What people or habits you want to let go of.
- What type of people you would like to meet.
- What places you would like to visit.

As you get more confident in your own decisions you can even decide:

- How you want to decorate your house.
- The type of films you would like to see.
- How you would like to dress.
- How you choose to relax.
- Whether you choose to have a clean or untidy house.
- Who you invite around.
- Who you don't invite around.
- How spontaneous you want to be.
- What you would like to watch on television.
- How you want to parent the children.

After a while you will so love making your own decisions, you will wonder how you ever lived the way you did. When you are ready you can make the choice whether you would like to invite another partner in to share your space.

CHAPTER 16
OMG I've handled it!

Going through a divorce or separation can be tough and challenging and drain you emotionally, physically and mentally. However I know you have the resources to handle the pain and you will get to a more positive place.

When you are at this positive place, you can then light the way for others and will be the beacon of strength they need to get through their own situation.

The lesson of separation will teach you many things about yourself, others and life. This is what life is all about, learning to move from a place of fear inside of us to a place of strength, love and compassion.

Letting go of the past is an important step forward. 'I Can Handle... Letting Go' will be a good book to read on your road to your journey to compassion for yourself and others.

Some of you after reading this book, may have decided that divorce or separation may not be the best option for you. Whatever decision you make, it has to be the right decision for you. All I ask, is that your final decision is made from a place of love for yourself and not from a place of fear. If you make your decision from a place of fear then this fear will always be inside of you. This fear makes us think we are not strong enough to handle anything that comes our way.

I know you have the power to handle whatever comes your way, in a loving and positive manner.

Are you ready to handle it?

Write your answers to these questions. Try and be as honest as you can. Remember the famous Russian proverb "It's better to be slapped by the truth than kissed by a lie". Being honest with yourself is the best option because "The loudest lie is the one you tell yourself".

What have you realised about your relationship?

e.g. I have settled and kept quiet as I like my house and lifestyle

What choices do you have to resolve this situation?

e.g. Depending on the financial situation I need to see how I could leave or ask her to leave

icanhandle **DIVORCE**

What is your action to resolve this situation?

e.g. 1. Contact a legal eagle 2. Speak to friend about it 3. See if I can get some free counselling

When will you do it by?

e.g. End of the month

Who will you tell you are going to do this so they can encourage you?

e.g. My best friend and parents

A personal message from Rachael Alexander

I applaud you for taking time to read this journable. I sincerely hope it has helped you think a little bit clearer and given you some strength to be able to move forward. When my marriage ended many years ago, I thought I could never feel emotional upset like it. I chose to walk away as I realised my marriage was not a healthy place for my son and I. When people ask me why I stayed for so long, I reply, because I thought I loved him. Even when we were arguing in court over finances I still felt as though I wanted to make it all better for him and I was selfish for making him go through this. I came to realise these feelings were born from thinking I didn't deserve to experience love from another, as I was not enough. I thought I was responsible for other people's happiness and my happiness didn't matter.

Through therapy, reading books and spiritual healing I now know that I am a lovable person worthy of love and respect. I may not know you personally dear reader but what I do know is that you too are worthy of being loved.

The separation journey is not an easy one, am I pleased I travelled it, a most definite yes! I learnt so much about the amount of strength and courage I have inside of me, and I know you will do the same.

Also, please remember sometimes it may not be a good idea to rush into a relationship with a new partner during or immediately after your separation. This is because the struggles in the old relationship often in time will get repeated in the new relationship. This is because until we have healed any old pent up pain from our past then the unresolved control dramas will play out in the new relationship. Making time for yourself and learning to enjoy being on your own helps you to feel more secure as you prove to yourself you don't need a significant other in your life. When you are ready you can then choose to accept another into your life. The Lyrics of Whitney Houston's Greatest Love of all gives great insight

> *"I decided long ago, never to walk in anyone's shadows*
> *If I fail, if I succeed*
> *At least I'll live as I believe*
> *No matter what they take from me*
> *They can't take away my dignity*
> *Because the greatest love of all*
> *Is happening to me*
> *I found the greatest love of all*
> *Inside of me*
> *The greatest love of all*
> *Is easy to achieve*
> *Learning to love yourself*
> *It is the greatest love of all"*

Let's enjoy the journey together of learning to love ourselves. Good luck, whatever your decision is.

From my courageous heart to yours.

Rachael Alexander

Other journables in the
I CAN HANDLE...Range

I Can Handle... Solutions for every life challenge - no matter what age you are